Cryptocurrencies and Blockchain Technology

A Full Guide About Trading and Investing Digital Cryptocurrencies and How to Potentially Make Money Off of It

Jeffrey Turpen

Your Gift!

We want to show our appreciation that you support our work, so we have put together a gift for you.

Just visit the link on the last page of this book to download it now.

We know you will love this gift.

Thanks!

Table of Content

DISCLAIMER	7
INTRODUCTION	8
CHAPTER 1 – UNDERSTANDING THE CRYPTOCURRENCY	9
General Features of Cryptocurrency	9
A Proof of Work Option	10
The Evolution of Cryptocurrency	11
What Can People Use it For?	12
CHAPTER 2 – BASIC POINTS ON CRYPTOCURRENCY	13
The Process of Mining Currency	13
Can You Mine on Your Own?	14
A Public Ledger Is Formed	15
The Address and the Key	16
The Transaction Process	17
Step By Step	17
Blockchain Support	18
The Security of Cryptocurrency	19

How Many Coins?	19
ABOUT No Intrinsic Value	20
Who Uses This Stuff?	21

CHAPTER 3 – THE PROS AND CONS OF CRYPTOCURRENCY — 22

Pros	22
Cons	24
About the Lack of a Centralized Body	24

CHAPTER 4 – TYPES OF CRYPTOCURRENCIES — 25

Bitcoin	25
Dash	26
Ethereum	26
Ripple	27
Litecoin	27
Dogecoin	28
A Few Extra Notes	28
But Do These Coins Do Anything?	29

CHAPTER 5 – HOW TO ACQUIRE YOUR CURRENCY — 30

| Get a Proper Wallet Ready | 30 |

Look For Exchanges	31
Managing Your Coins	32
Are Fees Involved With Transactions?	32
How Are You Identified?	33
How Much Time?	33
What About Reversals?	34
What About ICOs?	35

CHAPTER 6 – STORING YOUR CURRENCY   37

Cold Storage Works Best	37
Watch For Online Wallets	37
Use a Watch-Only Wallet	38
Personal Security Is Important	38

CHAPTER 7 – HOW ARE VALUES DETERMINED?   39

Node Count	39
Who Is Trading?	40
News Reports	40
Adoption Rates	41
Volume	42

CHAPTER 8 – READING A CRYPTOCURRENCY CHART   42

Supply Points	42
General History	43
Market Cap	43
Volume	44
Daily Reports	44
Individual Currency Markets	45
Always Analyze the Chart	45
Is the Value of Cryptocurrency Versus Real Money Important?	46

CHAPTER 9 – TIPS FOR INVESTING IN CRYPTOCURRENCIES — 47

Diversify Your Portfolio	47
Think of Them as Commodities	48
Remember How You Can Transfer Items	49
Prepare Goals	49
Watch For Stop Losses	49

FINAL WORDS — 50

Disclaimer

The following guide is all about cryptocurrencies including how they work and how you can invest in them. The information posted in this guide is useful and can help you get the most out of your investment plans if used right.

But like with any other investment out there, cryptocurrency is not a fully risk-free option. You are still risking financial losses when you have a cryptocurrency in your possession.

Be sure that you analyze everything relating to what you might want to invest in. Look at the values that come with your investment and see how it compares with other items you are working with in your portfolio.

Be aware of what is happening with whatever you are investing in as well. Look at the terms relating to your investment to see that what you are working with can be easy to handle.

Read the information in this guide to get a clear idea of how well cryptocurrencies can work. This is a very fascinating option for your investment desires but you should look at how well the process for acquiring currencies work and how these can be traded before you try getting into the market yourself.

Introduction

You have more than likely heard about people who invest in currencies. People often invest in currencies because they are valuable and distinct. Such investments are not as likely to be influenced by various outside factors as other options.

But not all currencies available for trading are tangible options. Today you can trade cryptocurrencies with other people from all corners of the world.

This is very different from other investment options for how it uses technology and a more complicated layout. But as you might find when you invest in it, this is a very distinct and fascinating option for your money needs that could work well.

A cryptocurrency is different from more traditional forms of currency. It is a peer-to-peer option that is decentralized. It is available with general transparency in mind.

Such currencies make transactions between parties a little easier to support. Others work without being overly difficult to spend money on.

Today you can invest in cryptocurrencies. These are available as strong options for your portfolio thanks to how distinct they are. They come in many forms and have different values that can change over time. The potential for you to make a profit by investing in such currencies is always out there.

But what it is about these currencies that make them special? It is understandable if you are not aware of how well a cryptocurrency works. It is a relatively new concept.

This guide will help you understand the many ins and outs that come with cryptocurrencies. You will see details on many intriguing points.

Details on how these currencies work and what they have to offer are important to notice. You will also learn about how to acquire and store such currencies. The information listed here is detailed and organized to help you understand the ins and outs that come with getting one of these currencies to work for your benefit.

You will be amazed at what you will get out of your plans for getting the most out of cryptocurrencies. But to make them work for you, it is vital for you to get a clear recognition of how they work.

Chapter 1 – Understanding the Cryptocurrency

The general definition of cryptocurrency is that it is a digital form of currency. It is named for how it uses cryptography to secure all transactions and to control how the currency develops.

The money is designed to stay safe and functional. This allows for money to be transferred well between people. The money could also work for general investments.

General Features of Cryptocurrency

A cryptocurrency is a virtual or digital form of currency. It is designed with a decentralized setup.

Such a currency is made through digital transactions. It is prepared with an extensive code that can be deciphered by people who have the proper keys for reading and reviewing that code.

The currency works with a payment network that uses a series of accounts and digital wallets. The digital money moves between individual parties.

The specific currency is also analyzed and recorded over time with extra bits of information on how well certain currencies are being moved around. This is a very simple type of currency that is intriguing and worthwhile for many demands.

The currency evolves over time as more people trade it. New coins are added based on how the mining process develops and how active people are with it. The values of such investments also change based on who is taking it in and how much it might be worth.

A Proof of Work Option

Cryptocurrency is designed as a proof of work solution for helping people get the most out of their currency investments. The proof of work system requires a computer user or program to make a strong effort when analyzing the currency in question. The proof of work in this case refers to how well a program identifies the individual features in the currency.

The general effort used here helps ensure that the currency is only read by the right parties. As this works, it provides you with proper information on how the currency is organized and what it takes to make it open and useful to the public.

The Evolution of Cryptocurrency

The concept of cryptocurrency first came along in the late 1990s. It was introduced as an electronic cash system where the transactions were anonymous and would entail a proof of work function. That is, the currency would be created by a complex computer program while coding is used to keep it secure and protected.

The Bit Gold program was the first such instance of cryptocurrency developed. But this was more of an experimental system used to test how well such a concept could work. The general goal was to find a way to make online transactions easier to handle with a currency that can work anywhere and is properly secured.

It was not until 2009 when cryptocurrency took a real turn. It was here that the Bitcoin came along. The currency used an advanced proof of work scheme while also being fully decentralized. Over the years the Bitcoin grew in popularity to where people could even acquire such coins through ATMs. The currency became popular for online transactions and eventually spawned many other currencies. Such currencies have especially been established for funding different projects with the intention of giving people huge profits down the line.

What Can People Use it For?

Cryptocurrency can be utilized in one of many special ways:

- It works with crowdfunding projects in mind. People who acquire coins can use them to help fund many larger projects that might be run by the groups that operate the coins.
- Many online retailers accept bitcoins. This is to simplify a transaction and make it work as quickly as possible.
- It is also ideal for many international transactions. Because cryptocurrencies are available throughout the world, there is no need to worry about exchange rates when paying for items with them. The values of items could vary though.
- Cryptocurrency also ensures that people can money sent out to the right people. The fact that it requires specific wallets that can read such coins makes it so the currency can actually be read by specific parties at a given time without risking any data being lost in the process.

Cryptocurrency is certainly something that deserves to be explored. It helps to look more to what is available on the market but you need to look at what is open first.

Chapter 2 – Basic Points on Cryptocurrency

There are a few basic aspects of cryptocurrency that deserve to be noticed. These relate to how well the currency can be produced. The ways how the currency can be used should be explored too as the details for making it work is rather intricate and complicated.

The Process of Mining Currency

To start, the cryptocurrency must be prepared with enough detail in mind. The mining process is extensive and tough but can work well if used right.

The currency used here is created through a process known as mining. This is where a computer resolves a math problem as a means of producing a coin or other bit of currency.

Anyone can produce a mining program. The cryptocurrency world is naturally open source so any kind of program could be set up. But the technical needs for getting it ready could be rather complicated as you are about to read.

Mining works as transactions are confirmed and calculated through a computer program. The program is often extremely extensive and complicated and requires a massive amount of disk space and processing power. In fact, many computers are built solely just to produce such currencies because of the immense power needed to produce something.

A computer that generates currency is extremely strong and operates with a powerful video card and processor. It also runs with a large amount of memory so it can produce the equations it needs for managing a strong setup. Software that analyzes the equation that must be resolved must also be added.

The mining process often produces multiple coins. A single block that is mined could include dozens of coins of the same currency. These could be used for many transactions.

The timing needed for the mining process to go through without any problems could be rather extensive. In some cases a miner only needs to spend a few minutes to get a coin ready. In other cases it might take hours or even days. The timing varies based on the design of the coin or how detailed the setup might be.

Can You Mine on Your Own?

Some cryptocurrency investors like to get the middleman out of the picture and mine their own coins. They do this to get coins that they can call their own and eventually sell for money.

But this process is generally for those who put in massive amounts of money just to get into the field.

Although you could order your own computer that produces currencies, the cost might be rather difficult to handle.

It would cost about $5,000 or more just to get a computer dedicated to producing cryptocurrencies. The fact that such computers are custom-made often makes them all the more complicated or hard to use. It would cost extra just to get such a computer made with specific parameters in mind.

In addition, it takes a while for coins to be mined. You might spend months just to get a single block prepared. This is due to the complicated process involved with producing such a block. You would also need a generator to keep your computer up and running. The process requires a great amount of continuous work. It could be reset if the power goes out. Don't forget about the cooling features and air circulation points needed to keep the computer from overheating.

In short, you could try and mine your own coins but that would cost thousands of dollars to do and would take a lengthy amount of time to complete. Sticking with general investments like what you will read about in this guide is the best way to go unless you have the technical knowledge and money to actually mine your own coins.

A Public Ledger Is Formed

As the individual coin or bit of currency is formed, a public ledger is added. The ledger lists information on the owner of the coin, any transactions made with that coin and so forth. The information is encrypted but it can be decoded by those who have the proper programs for using it.

This is utilized to ensure that the currency is transparent. People can find information on others who use a currency. Check the wallet you use to review individual coins that you hold. This is to give you a better idea of where your currency came from. Sometimes it might come from a newly mined coin but in other cases it would be from something that was utilized well in the past.

While it is true that individual names of people are not always listed, points on where something was used at could be incorporated into each block. This gives off enough points on how something was spent and used. Be aware of how well this is made when getting a good currency setup ready so you do not have less control than what you can use.

The Address and the Key

An address and a key are often used on cryptocurrencies. An address is the public information listed on the currency. It features a series of characters that identify the specific coin. The key is the private feature. It is a system that uses cryptography to keep the coin's specific bits of data secure and accessible only to those who have a proper key. This establishes control over the currency and will keep its data secure at all times.

Every individual coin has its own address and key. These create distinct coins that cannot be duplicated.

The public ledger also keeps tabs on all of these coins, thus ensuring nothing is counterfeit or used more than necessary. This is a part of the transparency that comes with cryptocurrency that makes it so ideal.

The Transaction Process

Transactions often take place between people who have wallets that support certain currencies. To make this work, two parties must have their own digital wallets.

The transaction from one digital wallet will go to a public ledger and then be confirmed. An encrypted signature adds information on the coin in terms of where it is going and when the deal is taking place. The process is used to ensure that the transaction is going from one actual person to the next.

It can take a few minutes for a cryptocurrency transaction to go through. It has to go through many keys and computers in a network to determine what is inside that coin. This ensures that the transaction is correct and that all information relating to what is used in the deal is fully accurate.

Step By Step

To understand more about the transaction process, it helps to look at the steps that go into it. These steps are used in the process to allow the transaction to move through and to get all the information associated with it recorded properly:

1. A person with a cryptocurrency will request a transaction.

2. The request is then sent to a network of peer-to-peer computers. These are known as nodes and are spots that support the currency in question.
3. The nodes will validate the transaction and confirm that the coins being used are authentic.
4. The transaction is then combined with others to add new data onto the coin. This creates the use of a new blockchain.
5. A new block is added to reflect upon the new transaction that was established.
6. The transaction is then completed.

This simple process takes a bit of time for it to work based on factors like the amount of money being moved and the type of currency. The number of nodes available to review the transaction will also make a difference.

Whatever happens here, the steps used will create a consistent approach to reviewing the currency being handled. This must all be reviewed well to see that the transaction being supported is managed the right way.

Blockchain Support

A distinct feature of cryptocurrency is that it features a blockchain. This is a list of records that relate to how the currency is used. It includes details on who owned the currency, how it has moved from one place to the next and so forth. The chain constantly grows over time based on the

individual transactions that develop. This special layout is convenient and easy to utilize.

This keeps information on a currency option to the public. It also prevents double spending, a process where the same digital money is spent more than one time.

Each block is permanent and cannot be altered. Such blocks are added after every new transaction that goes through. There are no limits as to how long such a block can be either. A larger size shows just how often the currency is being used and could influence how well the transaction in question moves.

The Security of Cryptocurrency

One of the most valuable features of cryptocurrency comes from how it is a fully secure and easy to use currency option. This is thanks to the cryptography used to produce it. Cryptography is a practice where codes are produced. Such codes are made to hide messages between parties. A key is used to decipher the code so it can be read in a simple language.

The layout of the coin in question is intricate and entails many bits of information to keep it safe. You will be excited at how well this is organized.

How Many Coins?

Like with any other currency in the world, there is a finite amount of cryptocurrencies. Each option out there is limited in terms of how many can be produced.

For instance, the Bitcoin currency has a limit to where only 21 million coins can be produced. The Litecoin system has a limit of 84 million coins.

The limit comes as the coding used for producing individual coins can only be so varied. The limitation is used to keep the coins from being counterfeited or duplicated in some illegal fashion.

This can be noticed when miners are producing new blocks that contain particular coins. As new blocks are produced, miners get fewer coins with each one. This eventually gets to the point where miners will hardly get anything.

However, the finite supply of such currencies would take a while to be satiated. It is estimated that the maximum number of Bitcoins that could be produced will not be reached until the middle part of the twenty-second century. Therefore, it would be easy for people to keep on getting currencies for as long as possible.

No Intrinsic Value

Unlike more traditional currencies, there are no intrinsic values associated with cryptocurrencies. All of these special currencies are designed to be digital-only. There are no physical currencies involved here.

That is, the Bitcoin is not an actual physical coin. All those images you see of people holding coins with the logo of a cryptocurrency on them are just demonstrations of what you could find.

The key point is that cryptocurrencies are not attached to government entities. The control that comes with such money is a little more open in nature.

This is a huge benefit as the currency is not at risk of being devalued by any government. It operates completely independently from government entities.

Governments often cause their currencies to become weaker in value. They do this to make their exports cheaper in value. This in turn makes it easier for their economics to grow although this is more of a theoretical point. Also, governments do this to make it so debtors will have a better chance with servicing their loans.

The threat of a government weakening its own money is always present. Cryptocurrencies are better for investments as they will not be touched by such large entities. This in turn reduces the overall risk associated with what you are working with.

Who Uses This Stuff?

Although cryptocurrencies are great to consider for your investment plans, you have to look at how popular they are in general. The truth is that while these are interesting, they are not necessarily as popular as you might think.

Coindesk, a prominent website that lists information on cryptocurrencies, states that around 15 million wallets for such currencies were in use at the start of 2017.

This is a high total but it is miniscule when in comparison with the number of people who could be investing.

Also, that total does not put into consideration how people can have more than one wallet each. Therefore, the actual number of people using such currencies is not bound to be overly high. But as the concept becomes more commonplace, more people are going to get their own wallets. The chances for currencies to be better investments will increase as more people learn about the market and get into it.

Cryptocurrency is certainly intriguing for everyone to take a look at. As you review your cryptocurrency, you will be surprised at how well it can work for your investment desire.

Chapter 3 – The Pros and Cons of Cryptocurrency

Cryptocurrency is a strikingly useful form of technology to see today. But it is also something that should be analyzed carefully based on how it can operate. There are some positive and negative aspects of cryptocurrency that deserve to be noticed.

Pros

- Cryptocurrencies protect people from payment fraud. Because of the intricate nature of such a currency and the extensive process used for confirming it, the risk of counterfeit currency being on the market is eliminated.

- The cryptocurrency field is fully open source. This means anyone could produce a program or wallet for reading currency programs.
- All information on the currency is open to those who have the proper keys for it. Since holders send information on the currency rather than have an outside party pull it, the information is protected well without identity theft being a threat.
- Any fees involved with sending out the currency will be minimal at best. Such fees refer to the process of buying a coin or using it for a transaction. The fees are generally cheaper than what you would spend on other payment methods.
- A payment with a currency only takes a few moments to go through. It does not require you to pay for something later on or to even be at risk of late payments or interest rates like with credit card transactions.
- Cryptocurrencies can be sent to anyone around the world including in places where more traditional exchange systems might not be easily accessible in.
- The fact that there are only a limited number of coins available makes them all the more valuable. These might offer inflation protection to customers just like with traditional precious metals.

Cons

- Some groups use cryptocurrencies to fund or purchase questionable items. While such currencies can be used for buying anything, many people like to use their currencies to order drugs, weapons and other items that are not supported by more traditional payment options.
- Technical issues and general human error can cause people to lose money. Those who hold this currency must be careful with it.
- Not all retailers or parties have access to cryptocurrency wallets or functions. This should be alleviated as the currency format becomes more commonplace.
- Prices for such currencies are based on supply and demand. The potential for the currency to change in value rather quickly is strong.

About the Lack of a Centralized Body

The fact that a cryptocurrency is made with no central entities for operating it is both a good and bad thing. On one hand, the currency is open to everyone and is made to be easily transferred and utilized.

On the other hand, the lack of centralization makes it to where a computer crash or other serious threat could cause the currency to be wiped out unless a proper backup is ready.

Be certain when looking at cryptocurrencies for investment purposes that you take a look at how they operate. These are appealing to find but they are not without risk.

Chapter 4 – Types of Cryptocurrencies

An exciting thing about cryptocurrencies is that they come in many forms. People are constantly creating their own currencies for many intentions.

Here are a few of the more appealing options you might find when investing in cryptocurrencies.

Bitcoin

Bitcoin is the mother of all cryptocurrencies – literally. It was the first cryptocurrency to be available for trading. It was introduced in 2009.

The currency option is popular for being very easy for anyone to acquire or trade. Bitcoin wallets are available for computers and mobile devices right now. It only takes a few moments to get one.

Also, the Bitcoin system is organized to where people can use it without understanding the complex or detailed technical bits of data that might come with it. This works for various transactions.

In addition, the Bitcoin system is more accessible than most other options. Much of this is thanks to the Bitcoin currency having been around for a while. You could find a payment card that you could physically carry around that links up to an online account that stores your Bitcoin totals. Still, not all people will accept the Bitcoin so be sure you look around to see what is available for your use.

Dash

Dash was created in 2014 as a more private version of Bitcoin. It uses a distributed code system that makes the information on the coin difficult to identify or trace. This makes it so people can use the currency without their information going around.

Ethereum

Ethereum was brought onto the market in 2015 as a currency that uses peer-to-peer transactions through a virtual machine. The system allows people to establish contracts where certain amounts of the currency can go from one party to the next in real time. This offers a simplified setup that is easy to operate with.

The blockchains within each Ether, which is the name of the coin used in the Ethereum system, are organized to where smart contracts are arranged.

The terms surrounding how coins are to be used are all listed within the currency. This ensures the user can make transactions with other parties without worrying about common problems where people are not familiar with one another in a transaction.

Ripple

Ripple is named for how it uses a public ledger system that uses a consensus through various basic functions. The special protocol used by Ripple requires more analysis for transactions as more parties will review the process. This ensures that the data being used is secure and safe to handle.

Litecoin

Litecoin is somewhat similar to Bitcoin in terms of how it is designed and utilized. With Litecoin, the code operates with an open source arrangement. The coins involved are not as valuable as what Bitcoin offers but they are still designed to be easy to manage and produce, thus making for an intriguing option for getting more out of a currency at any moment. Litecoin has a larger maximum total as up to 84 million units could be made in the life of the system. Meanwhile, it takes about two to three minutes for a block chain to be created in most instances. This uses a simplified process for getting the currency ready but it does not cost as much as a more traditional Bitcoin.

Dogecoin

Dogecoin is one option that has not gotten too much traction just yet but it is something that deserves to be noticed in the future. Dogecoin offers a target of 100 billion coins to be mined in its lifetime. About five billion of them were mined as of the start of 2017. Also, it takes about a minute for a block to be produced, thus making it easier for a coin to be mined.

The coin is being used with inflationary responses in mind. That is, a new series of coins will be produced based on how inflation develops on the market. The potential for more coins to come about in response to inflation could be an interesting feature that might impact how the commodity works.

A Few Extra Notes

What you have just read about are a few of the cryptocurrency options that you can find today. It would be difficult to mention every single one out there on the market right now. In September 2017, the Coin Market Cap website listed more than 1,100 digital currencies available for trading. Many were only getting off the ground while others were growing in prominence with nearly half of those currencies having a market cap of $100,000 or greater.

The site also said that in September 2017 the total market cap was around $125 billion. Close to half of that cap was held by the Bitcoin although Ethereum had close to a fifth of that total. The diverse array of currencies out there just shows how strong the industry is.

Feel free to look around online to see what other options are coming along. Considering how popular cryptocurrency has become over time, the odds are there are plenty of other choices for you to look at right now.

But Do These Coins Do Anything?

While these cryptocurrency options are all appealing, you have to look at what these coins can do in particular. The problem with so many currencies is that they are set up by people who just want to get money out of something.

The currencies that are posted out there just for the fun of it are likely to fall apart. They are choices that do not have many features for investors to work with.

Currencies designed with specific functions in mind are always more likely to succeed and more forward. Some are made to make banking functions more accessible in parts of the world where more traditional measures are not readily available. Meanwhile, others are designed to raise funds for schools, technical systems or more features made to help improve the lives of other people. These are more organized and made with strong layouts that will encourage growth. The money that comes from sales and the increases in their values will go towards supporting many of the positive functions a team wishes work with.

Look at the reasons that someone has for producing a currency. The groups that have a clear idea of what they want to do with their offerings and how they will produce a legitimate benefit over time are more likely to offer legitimate investments.

Be prepared to do your research into any group that offers a cryptocurrency. Always stick with the ones that have a clear idea of what they want to do.

Chapter 5 – How to Acquire Your Currency

When investing in cryptocurrency, you have to acquire it first. A few steps should be used when getting the most out of your currency so it will stay functional and useful for the desires you have. You must especially be safe while keeping your currency under control so it will not be problematic or hard to work with.

You can often find a currency right now although an initial coin offering could be utilized too. Both points are covered in this chapter.

Get a Proper Wallet Ready

To start investing in cryptocurrencies, you have to use a wallet. This is a digital program that lets you take in various currencies.

Such a wallet will operate with a basic layout that works well. You have to provide actual money to the wallet system. This allows you to have the funds needed for getting a transaction up and running.

You could connect your bank account or credit or debit card to your wallet. The key is to have something that includes real currency that can be converted into the new digital currency. There are limits as to how much you could spend on currencies. This is to keep the new money options under control and to ensure the demand is regulated well. This in turn keeps significant spikes in the value of certain coins from coming along.

You would have to confirm your identity to get your wallet prepared. A driver's license or other proof of information would have to be presented. The process confirms your identity and keeps the transaction safe.

Look For Exchanges

One place that you can find cryptocurrencies at is called an exchange. Such a place allows you to fund an account with a wallet and then acquire certain coins that can be spent or sold at a later time.

The exchanges you could find will vary based on where you live. In North America, you can use the Coinbase or BitFinex platforms. European users can use the Kraken or Bitcoin.de exchanges. BitFlyer and OKCoin are also noteworthy choices in Asia.

Whatever the case is, look at the terms associated with the place you want to get your currency at. Watch for how your native currency is treated too. The values between commonplace currencies like the American dollar, euro, British pound or Canadian dollar are all different and therefore will result in different totals to spend to acquire certain currencies.

Managing Your Coins

After you get your account with an online wallet supported, you will have to get money ready for transfer into certain currencies. A wallet should give you many options for acquiring your currency. Details on how many coins are good for whatever you have deposited should be listed.

In some cases you could take existing digital coins that you have and transfer them into other coins. This could add a great layout for making more money but you must watch for how the transfer process is used on your particular wallet. The coins should be kept under a secure network where the risk of items being stolen will be minimal.

Are Fees Involved With Transactions?

A great part of getting your new coins is that you will not have to bear with lots of high costs. The problem with so many traditional investments is that they entail high fees that might be worth a few percentage points. These fees eat away at any potential profits you might get.

With cryptocurrency exchanges, you will not bear with such high fees. The costs associated with each transaction are around 1 or 2 percent of the value of your deal at the most. This is a much more manageable total that can be afforded without real issues involved.

How Are You Identified?

You will not have your name sent out there when you get your transaction handled. This is different from more traditional investments in that your deal is measured based on the particular coin you have.

Coins come with their own individual addresses. The characters in such addresses might seem unusual and random, what with them having many letters and numbers, but each is designed to show which coin you are using. It keeps fraud and duplication from developing. It works as a good setup for your transactions while keeping your real world identity from being open.

How Much Time?

The process for getting such services for your needs will not take long for you to utilize. It should take about five to ten minutes for the transaction to be completed. It may take longer depending on how many nodes or levels of confirmation it must go through.

The time period is designed to allow it to go through a network and get as much information out as possible.

It does well for your use but there is one note that deserves to be seen in your transaction.

In many cases an investment might change in value between when you place an order and when it is finished. The currency might go up or down in value by a slight bit.

Fortunately, most places will lock in the value of your currency as the transaction is made. This means you are protected against any sudden changes in the value that may come about. Be certain to look at how well this can work when you are aiming to get a quality currency. You will not have to worry about sudden shifts in values when used right.

What About Reversals?

You must be extremely cautious when getting a transaction ready. All transactions with such currencies cannot be reversed.

This is important as you need to think about how well your deal will be made before you can go forward with it. All information that comes through with the transaction is final after it moves forward.

Watch for where you get the currency from too. You need to ensure that the person you take it from is authentic and has a pure identity without copying anything or stealing something from out of your account.

What About ICOs?

An ICO or initial coin offering is something to notice as well. This refers to the time period when a new cryptocurrency is offered by someone.

When an ICO takes place, the currency is just starting out. A series of coins will have already been mined in most cases. Only a few of them will be sent out to see that the coins can actually be sent out well.

In other cases you might simply be putting down money for coins that will be mined in the future. The ICO often helps gauge how prominent or popular an ICO might become.

An ICO could be found online through many providers. With this investment option being so popular, you might feel a desire to get right into the next ICO you see.

But an ICO is just like an IPO for a stock. You have to do your research before even getting into an offering.

Several tips should be used when getting into an ICO:

- Review where the ICO is coming from. Some groups might be a little more established than others. Those groups are easier to trust and support.
- Look at the values associated with the ICO. Are the values of the currency comparable with other options out there?
- See how the funding for the ICO was organized. Does the group working with the ICO have enough money to support the process?

- Review the endgame that the team with the offering wants to accomplish. Make sure the group you are getting the coins from have a real plan for the money it wants to raise or how it will handle the currency in the future.
- In the event that you are funding the process for mining, ask for details on how the mining process will work. A team needs the hardware and software needed for mining and a clear timetable for when your coins are to be made available to you.

Such an offering should be checked properly. There are plenty of ICOs popping up all the time with new investment options all around. Do look at how well these are organized so you will not get stuck with something unappealing or otherwise hard to follow.

More importantly, avoid any ICO from someone who is not all that open about what it going on with it. You need as much information on such a deal as possible before you even consider investing in it. You do not want to get into some transaction run by a scam artist.

Chapter 6 – Storing Your Currency

After you acquire your cryptocurrency, you will have to store it. A proper storage plan is needed to ensure you have enough protection for your investment and that what you are spending on it is appropriate.

Cold Storage Works Best

A cold storage plan for managing your currency is the best option to have. This keeps your currency safe and protected in the event of an outage or other drastic issue on a server.

Cold storage refers to keeping your currency offline. It is still valid but it will not be exposed at all times.

An offline cold storage wallet could be used in particular. A software program that saves information on your coins may work.

An offline storage media product could also work. A USB drive always works. The size of the currency is typically large so be sure you have a USB drive or other item that will secure your data for as long as possible.

Watch For Online Wallets

While many online wallets could be useful for helping you get your money spent and secured, you have to watch for any features that come with such wallets. The problem with many online wallets is that their information is regularly accessible. Seeing how such a currency is organized can be important to see.

You must see that the currency you use in particular is not hard to use or work with in any way. Look at how well your arrangement is laid out so you can get the most out of your wallet.

Use a Watch-Only Wallet

When getting a wallet ready on a mobile device or other computer, stick with a watch-only model. A watch-only wallet is one that lets you view your coin balance but does not allow you to spend your currency. This is a distinct option for your investment needs that protects you from spending your currency anywhere. It also keeps any information on your public device secured well enough.

Personal Security Is Important

The things you could do when getting your currency protected could be rather varied but it is even more important for you to look at how you are personally securing what you have. You should use a few tips:

- Review your transactions on private networks if possible. It is harder for people to break into secure private networks than if you tried to get on a public access network.
- Keep any login information for an account secure and away from other people. Do not make that information overly predictable either.

- Look at the security features of any website that you plan on accessing your coins with. A secure connection must be used at all times.

Be careful as you are storing your cryptocurrency. Watch for how you secure it and that you have a strong plan in hand for keeping it safe without any serious risks.

Chapter 7 – How Are Values Determined?

The potentials for the values of cryptocurrencies to be beneficial are great when you consider how they are not impacted by governments. But you must look at how well the values of individual currencies might come about.

You will notice when investing in cryptocurrencies that each one has its own particular value. Some currencies are worth a few dollars while others could go for thousands.

But what makes these currencies worth certain amounts of money? What makes them capable of increasing or decreasing in their values?

Each currency has its own value. Some currencies have coins worth hundreds or thousands of dollars. Others are just worth a few cents per coin.

Node Count

The node count for a cryptocurrency is important to review. This refers to the number of active wallets that are using such a currency at a time.

The more active currencies are more likely to have better

values as the demand for those coins are higher in value. Look at the blocks that are in the coins you acquire and you will see how active a currency might be. The ones that have larger blocks with more data are typically the most popular and appealing ones to see in terms of value.

Be advised that sometimes a person might have more than just one wallet dedicated to a certain investment. Therefore, the nodes that are open do not reflect the actual number of people working with a currency at a given moment.

Who Is Trading?

Many currencies increase in value when people keep on trading them. This comes as they are in increasing demand. With so many people aiming to trade those currencies, their values are bound to increase.

This measurement refers more to how many people have made transactions. This is regardless to the volumes of those transactions.

News Reports

Like with any other investment you might get into, news reports can make a huge difference. The news reports might entail points based on technology, economic information and much more. Anything that could influence the value of a currency should be reviewed as some stories might be more optimistic or pessimistic than others.

Of course, rumors can get in the way of some cryptocurrencies. The rumor of one currency pairing up with a tech partner or other special entity might cause the value of that currency to increase after a while.

But you must be careful when such rumors come about. Sometimes those rumors end up leading to unverified information. This makes it harder for you to get the investments that you want to come with values that are easy to follow.

It is easier to find news stories relating to your currency online. Look around many websites to get details on what is open so you can get the most out of your investment. You will notice when investing that the online world is a better source for information simply because most major media outlets have not necessarily focused on this subject just yet.

Adoption Rates

The rate of adoption for a cryptocurrency is important to see. It is easier for currencies to gain a bit of extra traction when they are being used by more people at a given time. When your coin is used by more people, its value will increase thanks to the strong adoption that comes with it. People will be more interested in the currency as they are likely to start trading it. Plenty of media exposure and work for developing the currency should take place for a currency to be adopted properly. Look at what news stories have come along with such an option and see if they are prompting people to invest in it.

Volume

The volume of a coin is important to note. Some coins tend to be further along as they are working with more coins at a given time. Such coins are more appealing and worth getting into for your investment demands.

But you should look at how well the volume is read. The volume refers to the number of coins that are being transferred. This includes how many are spent at a certain time or how many people are buying. Look at this and see what factors might have caused the volume to change at some point.

Be sure to look at what can happen with any cryptocurrency you wish to invest in. Remember that all such currencies can be influenced by many factors. Check around carefully to see what the values of certain currencies are.

Chapter 8 – Reading a Cryptocurrency Chart

As you invest in particular cryptocurrencies, you will notice a good number of points in each listing. You must look at several things when you are trying to invest in such a currency.

Supply Points

A chart should include information on the supply available for a coin.

The information should include points on how many coins have been mined at a given time.

Details on the rate at which new coins are being produced should be listed as well. This gives you an ideal of whether an option is actually active or if it is dormant.

The maximum supply should be included as well. This refers to the total number of coins that could be mined in the lifespan of the currency. It would take several lifetimes for a currency to get to that maximum supply but it helps to get an idea of how well the production process for a currency is going.

General History

The history of a currency should be checked well. In most cases you can notice this by looking at the chart showing how the value of that currency has changed over time.

You could notice when the currency first became available based on how far back that chart goes. But even with this, you should look at how much people spent at the beginning to get an idea of how committed people might have been towards a certain investment option.

Market Cap

The market cap of a currency refers to its value at a certain period of time. Naturally, the value of the currency is higher when the market cap is greater.

When the cap changes, it means that people are buying or selling a certain currency. They are working with different plans for using certain currencies at this rate.

Volume

The volume is the total amount of currency being traded within a period of time. It is typically measured based on the last 24 hours.

The volume could change for many reasons. It might change due to big news or developments surrounding a currency. It may also go up or down following certain transactions. Look carefully at how the volume and see why it has changed.

The potential for the value to change would be higher when the volume is greater. In particular, the largest gains or drops come when more people are trading at a certain time. But in most cases the volume would be consistent without many lulls or spikes.

Do look at the chart to figure out what could have happened at a given time when the volume really changed beyond its normal rate. There is always a good reason for why something is happening.

Daily Reports

Daily reports show how the value of something changed in a 24-hour period. It shows the opening and closing values of something alongside the highest and lowest totals associated with the item.

This is similar to what you might see when investing in trading options. You might see charts that reveal how the peaks and valleys of some investment changed over time.

Reading such reports gives you a look at whether people have limits in terms of how much they would spend on the currencies they take in. Look at these limits to get a clear idea of what might come about as you are getting an investment ready.

Individual Currency Markets

Currency markets are good to notice. These refer to cases where a particular currency is being traded through certain channels or markets. They may also entail people transferring one currency to another.

The ways how people take in currencies speak volumes on how people are using them. You might find some that are gathered by people who also invest in certain items. The individual portals that people reach currencies with could also be checked. See how well the behaviors of people who buy these currencies are so you can find something that stands out and has a good layout.

Always Analyze the Chart

Be certain when looking at a cryptocurrency that you review the chart attached to it. The chart lists points on how much money the currency is worth and when it has become more popular. Look at how the value of a currency has changed and what made its value go up or down.

Think about any trends that might come about within an investment as some might be trending upward or downward.

The analysis you would use should be similar to what you would get out of any other investment you might choose. Review the points listed on your currency and make sure it is carefully managed without being hard to follow in some way.

Is the Value of Cryptocurrency Versus Real Money Important?

There is an important additional point you need to review when getting a currency ready in your portfolio. This relate to how the new form of money links up with something a little more established and familiar to people.

One thing you might notice when acquiring cryptocurrencies is that you would have to spend a certain amount of real money to get them. In particular, you might read stories about the Bitcoin being compared with the American dollar.

But does that mean cryptocurrencies are to be compared with real money?

The value of the cryptocurrency in comparison with an actual physical currency is often measured as a general analysis of the digital currency in some form. That is, it shows how strong the new currency is when compared with something a little more traditional.

When the Bitcoin is listed as being worth a few thousand American dollars, it means that the Bitcoin is growing in power. It is just valuable and treated well in comparison with the American dollar. This does not mean that the Bitcoin is definitely worth that total.

Still, you must look at what you could acquire when getting onto an exchange for finding such currencies. The potential for you to spend a massive amount of money on such a currency is still strong when everything about it is considered.

Be careful as you look at the points relating to whatever you want to invest in. All currencies operate differently and must be reviewed well for your benefit. You will have a better chance with getting more out of your work if you think about how something could be utilized.

Chapter 9 – Tips For Investing in Cryptocurrencies

As you invest in cryptocurrencies, you will come across many options that might be of value to you. But when looking for such currencies, you have to use a few pointers for getting a quality currency investment up and running for your personal requirements.

Diversify Your Portfolio

While there are some currencies that are clearly more popular than others, you should still invest in many options. Stick with multiple currencies when getting your portfolio ready. Diversification entails working with a variety of investment options. These would entail many options in different fields or setups. The goal of diversification is to reduce the overall risk associated with certain investments.

Investing in just one option is never a good idea as you would be putting in far too much work into a certain choice. Working with many investment options is always worthwhile. Sticking with enough choices is great as you will keep from being overly reliant on just one. This gives you a little more control over the risks you are putting yourself into.

Do not go into overkill when you are trying to get these currencies though. Pick a few that you know are of use to you and keep your portfolio under control without adding more than needed. Only look at what you know is easy to actually invest in so you will have more out of what you wish to invest in.

Think of Them as Commodities

One way to invest in cryptocurrencies is to think of them as if they were commodities. It is true that currencies are different from oil, livestock, crops or other more traditional commodities. But the values of these currencies change in the same way that such investments might change.

They go up and down in value based on market sentiments, scarcity and demand. The chances for anything to grow in value are always strong but you should at least look at what goes into an investment before choosing something that you know fits your needs.

Review the charts for each choice too. Note how their daily values could be compared just as well as anything else of value to you.

Remember How You Can Transfer Items

You can always transfer your cryptocurrencies into other currency options as you see fit. Be aware of what you could get into when transferring your currency into something else though.

You can get your money transferred into actual American dollars or another currency that you might regularly use. Do check on the value that you will get and compare it with what you spent on the currency in the first place. You do not want to feel ripped off by selling it for less than what you bought it for. Then again, it does take time in many cases for such currencies to become a little more valuable.

Prepare Goals

Every transaction you put in should have its own goal. A great goal could be to have something move up to a specific value. Look at the objectives you have for each deal you make. Create more realistic ones that are easy to follow.

Be aware that it might take a while for some of those goals to come true. Thinking with long term efforts in mind may be worthwhile as it gives you extra control over what you are aiming to invest in.

Watch For Stop Losses

Stop losses can be prepared in any deal you make. This is where you would sell your currency if it gets to a certain value that is too low.

A stop loss order keeps you from losing more than what you can afford. Even with that in mind, you must keep the loss total from being too deep. Keep the stop loss set at about 20 percent less than the value of what you originally took in. This is just a sample option but it does fit in well with the investment you wish to use.

Be aware of what you are doing as you invest in a cryptocurrency. Do not stick with something that might be too hard to work with or else you would be at risk of losing far too much money.

Final Words

Cryptocurrency is very interesting to see when it comes to your investments. This special type of investment is exciting for how it provides you with many ways to make money.

The distinct features of cryptocurrencies make them easy to trade and ideal for many investment demands. The variety of currencies that you could use especially makes for something all the more fascinating.

But when looking for great currencies, you have to look at what is available for your use. See how well it can be held and how it is mined. Look at what makes the currency of interest to you stand out.

More importantly, be careful when investing in any kind of cryptocurrency.

The chances for you to get some huge payouts off of an investment like this could be strong. Of course, these currencies are useful for spending on their own but you must look at the points associated with getting one of these ready. Good luck and have fun with your investment plans. You will be excited to see how well such investments can work in your portfolio.

Your Gift!

We want to show our appreciation that you support our work, so we have put together a gift for you.

bit.ly/2xXbHO5

Just visit the link above to download it now.

We know you will love this gift.
Thanks!

www.ingramcontent.com/pod-product-compliance
Lightning Source LLC
Chambersburg PA
CBHW050245230526

45470CB00005B/2122